Arizona Tr ␣ Introduction

This book is part of the *Easy Field* ␣ bout common plants, critters, and fossil ␣ ntire Southwest. We think you will find ␣ new kinds of trees. A checklist is include ␣ rd of the trees you observe.

MW00438158

We have selected forty-seven of the most common species of trees to include in this guide. Included are those characteristics and facts which we feel you will find particularly useful in identifying the tree in question. Keep in mind that all leaves, even those from the same tree, may show some variation.

Since elevations in Arizona range from about sea level in the southwestern deserts to over 12,000 feet at the highest point, there are many different habitats for trees. This is reflected in a great variety of trees, from the Ironwood which grows only in frost-free areas to old Bristlecone Pines which grow near the timberline. Arizona's State Tree is the Palo Verde.

Honey Mesquite:

Leaves with 9-or-more pairs of small leaflets; twigs with stout, paired, yellowish spines; note the shape of the 4-to-7-inch pod; abundant along desert washes and grasslands; compare with Screw Bean Mesquite and Ironwood; sea level to 4,000 feet.

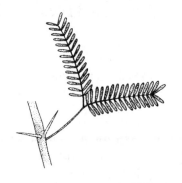

Screw Bean Mesquite:

Leaves with 8-or-less pairs of small leaflets; twigs with thin, white paired spines; pods are spiral shaped, up to 2-inches long; compare with Honey Mesquite and Ironwood; sea level to 4,000 feet.

Ironwood:

Leaves with paired, gray-colored leaflets; each leaflet is less than ¾-inch long; compare with green-barked Palo Verdes and Mesquites; usually keeps leaves all year, other similar-appearing trees don't; pods are hairy with only a few constrictions; usually found along washes, 500-2,500 feet.

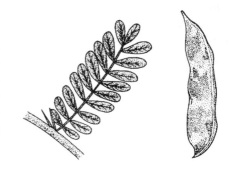

New Mexican Locust:

Large shrub or small tree; leaves 8-to-12-inches long, with 13-or-more leaflets; leaflet is less than 1½-inches long with small point at the end; stems with paired spines; up to 4-inch long flat pods; mountains, 5,000-8,000 feet.

Foothill Palo Verde:

Young stems and parts of bark are yellow-green; leaflets, when present, are less than 1/8-inch long; leaflets usually have 4-or-more pairs on each tiny stem; pods constricted between seeds and with point at tip; common in deserts, 1,000-3,500 feet.

Blue Palo Verde:

Young stems have bluish-green bark; leaflets, when present, are usually more than 1/8-inch long, with 3-or-less pairs of leaflets on each tiny stem; pod is somewhat flattened, but not greatly constricted; desert washes, sea level to 3,500 feet.

Arizona Sycamore:
Large leaves 5-to-9-inches long and wide with star-like shape; whitish bark; picturesque spreading branches; ball-shaped fruits have long stems and are often found dried on the ground; common tree along creeks, 2,500-6,500 feet.

Netleaf Hackberry:

Leaves have "off-center" somewhat heart-shaped appearance; 1-to-3-inch leaves usually have 3 main veins coming from stem; top of leaf coarse to touch, bottom with raised veins; small tree; along washes, 2,000-5,500 feet.

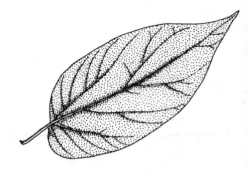

Common Chokecherry:

Leaf about 3-inches long; top darker than bottom; leaf edges with teeth; reddish fruit with large seed; small tree along streams in mountains, 5,000-7,500 feet.

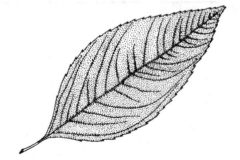

Arizona Mandrone:

Leaves spear-shaped, thick, 1-to-2½-inches long, some with smooth edges, others have small teeth; distinctive bark is reddish color and very thin, usually peeling; mountains of Arizona, 4,500-7,500 feet.

Velvet Ash:

Leaf divided into 5-to-8 leaflets, each leaflet 1-to-2½-inches long; distinctive seed has a long wing on it; seed plus wing about 1-inch long; seeds are not paired but occur in groups; along creeks, 2,500-6,500 feet.

Desert Willow:
Distinctive leaves very long in relation to width, often more than 5-inches long and less than ½-inch wide; seed pods also long, often as long or longer than leaves and as little as ¼-inch in diameter; pods stay on all winter; desert washes, 2,000-4,500 feet.

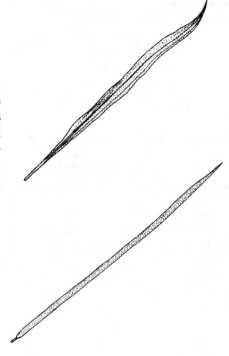

Arizona Cypress:

small scale-like leaves; round cones about ¾-inch diameter, divided into sections, each with a small mound on it; bark grayish with vertical "scars;" can be large tree; along creeks in mountain canyons, 4,000-7,000 feet.

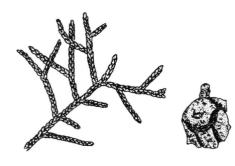

California Fan Palm:

Grows in the wild, in Palm Canyon in the Kofa Mountains south of Quartzsite; our only species of native palm; all other palms are introduced; leaves about 5-feet long, fan shaped; 2,500 feet.

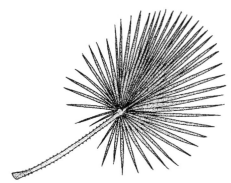

One Seed Juniper:

Small scale-like leaves; distinguished from Utah and Rocky Mountain Junipers because: usually smaller tree with many small trunks coming from below or near ground level; lacks a single main trunk; purplish-blue berries ¼-inch diameter with only 1 seed and usually juicy; berries on females, pollen on males; 3,000-7,000 feet.

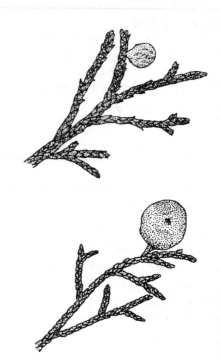

Utah Juniper:

Small scale-like leaves; has single main trunk with branches starting lower than the Rocky Mountain Juniper; berries fibrous inside; 3,500-7,000 feet.

Alligator Juniper:

Small scale-like leaves; distinctive bark divided into "squares" resembling back of an alligator; berry about ½-inch diameter and grayish-green; mountains, 4,000-7,000 feet.

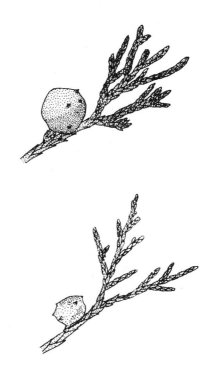

Rocky Mountain Juniper:

Small scale-like leaves; usually a single, main trunk; ¼-inch bluish berry usually with 2 seeds, and juicy when squeezed; flattened tips of small branchlets hanging down; 5,500-8,500 feet.

Arizona Walnut:

Leaf about 12-inches long with 10-or-more leaflets coming off main stem; each leaflet about 3-inches long and 1-inch wide; look for walnuts on ground; these have a fibrous outer husk and a hard inner shell; along streams and washes, 4,000-6,000 feet.

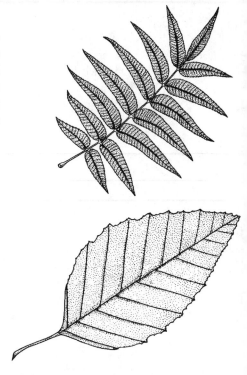

Arizona Alder:

Leaves about 3-inches long; edges with small teeth; small "cones" about ½-inch long; common along banks of creeks, 5,000-6,000 feet.

Narrowleaf Hoptree:

Leaves with 3 leaflets; leaflets are 1-to-2½-inches long; surface of leaflets has tiny glands which emit a strong odor; seed with flattened, rounded wing and small stalk; seed plus wings about ½-inch across; small tree in mountain canyons, 4,000-8,000 feet.

Inland Box Elder:

Leaves with 3 or 5 leaflets, the middle leaflets on a stalk; leaflets 3-to-4-inches long and edges with large teeth; seeds in pairs with wings; along creeks in canyons and mountains, 4,000-7,000 feet.

Rocky Mountain Maple:

Two types of leaves may be present—one undivided, the other divided into 3 leaflets where leaf edges have big teeth with smaller teeth on them; leaves turn red in autumn; seeds in pairs with wings; along creeks in pine forests, 7,500-9,000 feet.

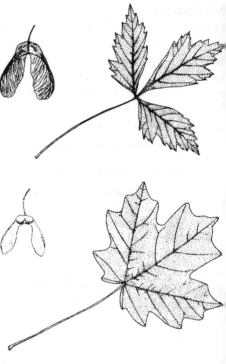

Bigtooth Maple:

Leaves 3-to-5-inches long; each leaf with 3 main lobes; points on leaves are blunt; leaves thicker than those of Rocky Mountain Maple; seeds in pairs with wings; pine forests, 5,000-7,500 feet.

Mexican Blue Oak:

Leaves with distinctive oblong shape, about 1½-inches long; ends of leaves rounded and base indented; tops of leaves often a bluish-green color; southern Arizona mountains, 5,000-6,000 feet.

Gray Oak also called Scrub Oak:

Leaves up to 1½-inches long, pointed at tip, somewhat heart-shaped; leaf edge usually smooth; top of leaf shiny, bottom somewhat hairy; 5,000-6,000 feet.

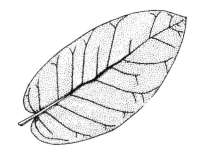

Gambel Oak:

Leaves with distinctive lobes; leaves about 3-to-6-inches long; unlike our other oaks, loses leaves in winter; common small tree on cool mountain slopes, especially Oak Creek Canyon; 5,000-7,500 feet.

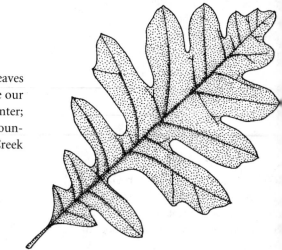

Netleaf Oak:
Leaves about 3-inches long, very thick and leathery; bottom of leaf concave with distinct raised veins; top of leaf dark green (compare with lighter Arizona White Oak); in canyons, 4,000-6,000 feet.

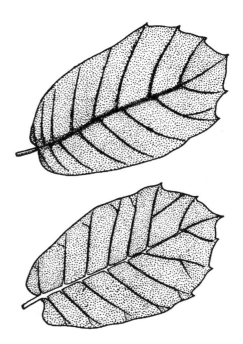

Arizona White Oak:
Leaves similar to those of Netleaf Oak, but proportionately Arizona White Oak leaves are usually more than twice as long as wide—those of Netleaf less; leaf often thick and somewhat leathery as with Netleaf; top of leaf light green; 5,000-7,000 feet.

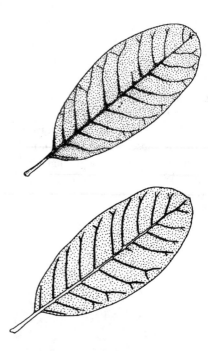

Emory Oak:
Leaves 1-to-2½-inches long; edges often have a few sharp teeth or smooth edges (both leaf types often on same tree); both top and bottom of leaf shiny; two fuzzy spots at base of leaf on bottom; very common in southern Arizona mountains, 4,000-6,500 feet.

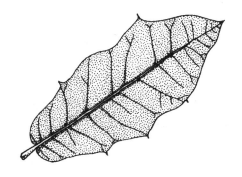

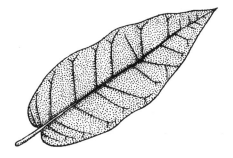

Silverleaf Oak:
Leaves spear-shaped, pointed at tip; leaves 3-to-4-inches long, about ¾-inch wide; tops of leaves green, bottoms a fuzzy white (silver); edges of leaves curl under; common in mountains, 5,500-7,500 feet.

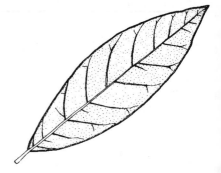

Narrowleaf Cottonwood:

Leaves spear-shaped; leaf length 3-to-4-inches, usually less than 1-inch wide; leaf edges with fine teeth; often large tree; along creeks, 5,000-8,000 feet.

Fremont Cottonwood:

Triangular-shaped leaves with long, flattened stems; leaf edges with uneven teeth; very common, large tree along streams at lower elevations, sea level to 6,000 feet.

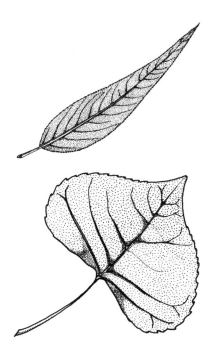

Quaking Aspen:
Leaves roundish with long stems which are flattened from side-to-side where they join the leaf blade; bark whitish; leaves flutter in slight breezes; forms beautiful gold and yellow autumn colors; grows on cool mountain slopes, 7,000-9,500 feet.

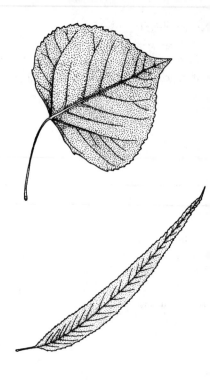

Goodding Willow:
Largest of the many species of willows found in Arizona; narrow leaves 3-to-5-inches long, about ½-inch wide; along streams, sea level to 6,000 feet.

Mexican Pinyon (Pine):
Needles 1½-inches long in groups of 3; typical pinyon cone about 1-inch high; small tree common in southeastern Arizona mountains, 5,000-7,000 feet.

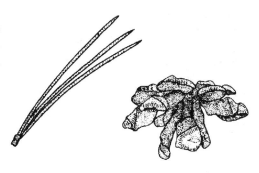

Colorado Pinyon (Pine):
Needles 1½-inches long in groups of 2; cone contains edible seeds (pine nuts); common on south rim of Grand Canyon and in northern Arizona, 5,000-7,000 feet.

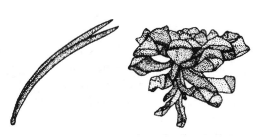

Singleleaf Pinyon (Pine):
Single needle 1½-inches long; cone larger than those of the other pinions; similar to Colorado Pinyon; scattered localities in northern Arizona, 4,000-6,000 feet.

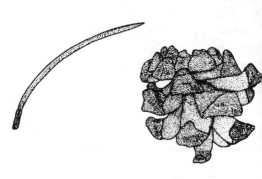

Bristlecone Pine:
Needles ¾-inch long in groups of 5; purplish cones about 3-inches long; small, sharp structures on cones; found along San Francisco Peaks in northern Arizona from about 9,000 feet to timberline.

Chihuahua Pine:

Needles 3-to-4-inches long in groups of 3; somewhat resembles longer-needled Ponderosa Pine; needle groups which have fallen to the ground have lost their sheaths while those of the Ponderosa Pine haven't; needles of the Chihuahua Pine are thinner than those of Ponderosas; cones have definite stalks and remain on the tree for long periods; mountains of southeastern Arizona, 5,000-7,000 feet.

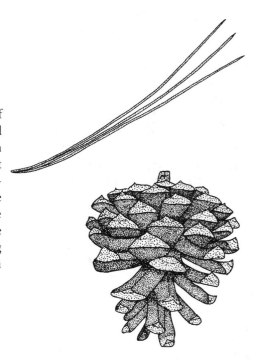

Ponderosa Pine:
Needles 5-to-7-inches long in groups of 3, 4, or 5; abundant, often very large tree; occurs in huge stands; bark reddish-brown with puzzle-like appearance of flaking bark when viewed closely; compare with less common Chihuahua and Apache Pines; 5,000-7,500 feet.

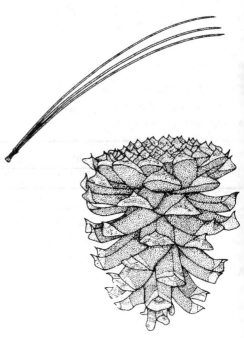

Apache Pine:

Very long needles (10-inches or more) in groups of 3; needles often wider than those of Ponderosa Pine; tree often appears similar to Ponderosa Pine, but in addition to longer and wider needles, the sheaths around the needles of Apache Pine are often ¾-inch or longer, those of Ponderosa Pine are less; mountains and canyons of southeastern Arizona, 5,000-7,000 feet.

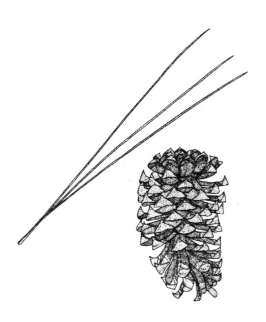

Limber Pine:
Needles 2½-inches long in groups of 5; very large cones (about 6-inches long); no sharp points on cones; common in mountains, 6,000-10,000 feet.

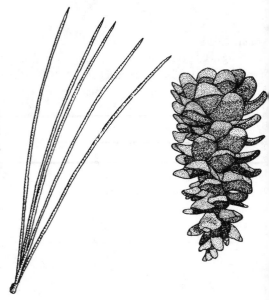

Douglas Fir:

Needles 1-inch long; needles flattened and with a thin indentation running the length on top; cones distinctive, with 3-pointed structure sticking out between scales; cones about 2-inches long; cool mountain areas, 6,000-10,000 feet.

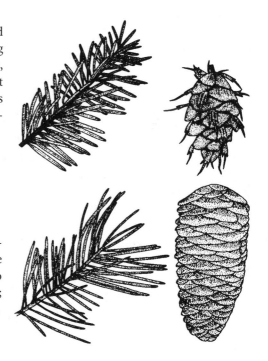

White Fir:

Needles 1-to-3-inches long; where flat-ened needles attach to twigs they have a sucker-like appearance; cones fall to pieces when mature; often small tree; cool mountain areas, 6,000-9,000 feet.

Engelmann Spruce:

Needles 4-sided, about ¾-inch long with a sharp tip; small twigs have bumps on them where needles are attached; the cones are 2-inches long with thin scales; high mountains, 8,500 feet to timberline.

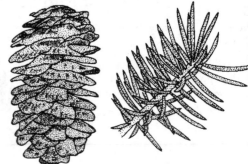

Alpine Fir:

Needles 1½-inches long, tending to be fatter toward their bases; upright, purplish cones on the tree are the easiest means of identification; cones 3-inches long but fall apart while still on the tree; high mountains, 8,000 feet to timberline.

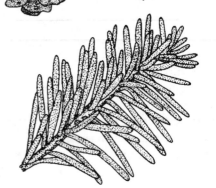

Checklist And Scientific Names

- ☐ Alligator Juniper – *Juniperus deppeana* 11
- ☐ Alpine Fir – *Abies lasiocarpa* 30
- ☐ Apache Pine – *Pinus latifolia* 27
- ☐ Arizona Alder – *Alnus oblongifolia* 12
- ☐ Arizona Cypress – *Cupressus arizonica* 9
- ☐ Arizona Madrone – *Arbutus arizonica* 7
- ☐ Arizona Sycamore – *Platanus wrightii* 5
- ☐ Arizona Walnut – *Juglans major* 12
- ☐ Arizona White Oak – *Quercus arizonica* 18
- ☐ Bigtooth Maple – *Acer grandidentatum* 14
- ☐ Blue Palo Verde – *Cercidium floridum* 3
- ☐ Bristlecone Pine – *Pinus aristata* 24
- ☐ California Fan Palm – *Washingtonia filifera* 9
- ☐ Chihuahua Pine – *Pinus chihuahuana* 25
- ☐ Colorado Pinyon – *Pinus edulis* 23
- ☐ Common Chokecherry – *Prunus virginiana* 6
- ☐ Desert Willow – *Chilopsis linearis* 8
- ☐ Douglas Fir – *Pseudotsuga taxifolia* 29
- ☐ Emory Oak – *Quercus emoryi* 19
- ☐ Engelmann Spruce – *Picea engelmanni* 30
- ☐ Foothill Palo Verde – *Cercidium microphyllum* 3
- ☐ Fremont Cottonwood – *Populus fremontii* 21
- ☐ Gambel Oak – *Quercus gambelii* 16
- ☐ Goodding Willow – *Salix gooddingii* 22

Checklist and Scientific Names

- [ ] Gray Oak – *Quercus grisea* — 15
- [ ] Honey Mesquite – *Prosopis julifora* — 2
- [ ] Inland Box Elder – *Acer negundo* — 13
- [ ] Ironwood – *Olneya tesota* — 4
- [ ] Limber Pine – *Pinus flexilis* — 28
- [ ] Mexican Blue Oak – *Quercus oblongifolia* — 15
- [ ] Mexican Pinyon – *Pinus cembroides* — 23
- [ ] Narrowleaf Cottonwood – *Populus angustifolia* — 21
- [ ] Narrowleaf Hoptree – *Ptelea angustifolia* — 13
- [ ] Netleaf Hackberry – *Celtis reticulata* — 6
- [ ] Netleaf Oak – *Quercus reticulata* — 17
- [ ] New Mexican Locust – *Robinia neomexicana* — 4
- [ ] One Seed Juniper – *Juniperus monosperma* — 10
- [ ] Ponderosa Pine – *Pinus ponderosa* — 26
- [ ] Quaking Aspen – *Populus tremuloides* — 22
- [ ] Rocky Mountain Juniper – *Juniperus scopulorum* — 11
- [ ] Rocky Mountain Maple – *Acer glabrum* — 14
- [ ] Scredown; 5,500-8,500*Prosopis pubescens* — 2
- [ ] Silverleaf Oak – *Quercus hypoleucoides* — 20
- [ ] Singleleaf Pinyon – *Pinus monophylla* — 24
- [ ] Utah Juniper – *Juniperus osteosperma* — 10
- [ ] Velvet Ash – *Fraxinus velutina* — 7
- [ ] White Fir – *Abies concolor* — 29